Doreen Kupke

Runtriz - The Leader of mobile Hospitality

Hotel Evolution

GRIN Verlag

Bibliografische Information der Deutschen Nationalbibliothek:

Die Deutsche Bibliothek verzeichnet diese Publikation in der Deutschen National-
bibliografie; detaillierte bibliografische Daten sind im Internet über http://dnb.d-
nb.de/ abrufbar.

Imprint:

Copyright © 2012 GRIN Verlag GmbH
Druck und Bindung: Books on Demand GmbH, Norderstedt Germany
ISBN: 978-3-656-38464-9

This book at GRIN:

http://www.grin.com/en/e-book/210444/runtriz-the-leader-of-mobile-hospitality

GRIN - Your knowledge has value

Der GRIN Verlag publiziert seit 1998 wissenschaftliche Arbeiten von Studenten, Hochschullehrern und anderen Akademikern als eBook und gedrucktes Buch. Die Verlagswebsite www.grin.com ist die ideale Plattform zur Veröffentlichung von Hausarbeiten, Abschlussarbeiten, wissenschaftlichen Aufsätzen, Dissertationen und Fachbüchern.

Visit us on the internet:

http://www.grin.com/

http://www.facebook.com/grincom

http://www.twitter.com/grin_com

Runtriz- The Leader of mobile Hospitality

by Doreen Kupke

**Assignment Paper for the Master´s degree class of
Service Innovation**

Lectured by

Due Date 17th of October
Karlstad University

Table of contents

(I) List of figures and tables 1

(II) List of abbreviations 1

1. Introduction... 2

  1.1 Background and Purpose of the Topic 2

  1.2 Methodology... 2

2. Case Description 3

  2.1 The History of Runtriz.. 3

  2.2 Introduction of the Invention Hotel Evolution 3

3. Theory.. 5

  3.1 Definition of Service Innovation 5

  3.2 Service Innovation Models 5

    3.2.1 Models from Gallouj and Weinstein.. 5

    3.2.2 Models from Michel, Brown and Gallan...................................... 6

4. Case Analyses 7

  4.1 Radical Innovation... 7

  4.2 Incremental Innovation 8

  4.3 Changing the Customer Roles and Firm`s Value Creation................ 9

5. Conclusion 11

(III) List of references.. 12

(I) List of figures and tables

Figure 1: Changing the Customer Roles and Firm`s Value Creation........................ 10

(II) List of abbreviations

app   application

etc.   et cetera

S-D logic   Service-Dominant logic

Runtriz- The Leader in mobile Hospitality | Due Date
by Doreen Kupke | 17th of
October

1. Introduction

1.1 Background and Purpose of the Topic

The service industry, especially the hospitality industry, has to handle high pressure from competition and frequently changing demands from their customers (Victorino et al., 2005). Hotels have to establish a unique offering or service for their guests, to highlight themselves on the market. A way to generate a successful establishment within the hospitality industry is to implement and develop innovations, which can be seen as the creation of an extra value for the guest (Victorino et al., 2005). Findings from various articles and books like *Service innovation and customer choices in the hospitality industry* from Victorino et al. in 2005 and *Open Services and Innovation* from Henry Chesbrough in 2011, lining out that Service Innovations have an impact on the choice of customers and are a *"clear and sustainable way to grow a business"* (Chesbrough, 2011, p.13). Therefore, innovations have been coming into focus of importance also in the hospitality industry. (Victorino et al., 2005)

Runtriz, a company from the United States, has specialized itself in offering mobile solutions for luxury hotels. Their newest invention is called Hotel Evolution and was brought at the market in 2008. Hotel Evolution is a mobile touch screen platform, which allows guests to communicate and interact with the staff in the hotels (Enz et al., 2010). The question arising is what is the actual innovation of Hotel Evolution. Therefore, the overall aim is the analysis of the innovation, Hotel Evolution. Different theories and models will be used to apply the chosen case with scientific theory.

1.2 Methodology

The report will be based firstly on a short illustration from the chosen company and their innovation, to have a good starting base for the later discussion, analysis and the solution finding. Secondly, different Service Innovations and models will be described and a definition of the term Service Innovation will be done in chapter 3. Thirdly, the chosen theories and models will be connected with the case of the innovation, Hotel Evolution.

A literature conducted analyze is used to gain the theoretical knowledge. The usage of different studies, professional articles and internet sources, shall help to achieve a direct connection between theory and practice.

Runtriz- The Leader in mobile Hospitality | Due Date
by Doreen Kupke | 17th of
October

2. Case Description

2.1 The History of Runtriz

"The hospitality industry had not fully grasped opportunities that modern technology provides and customers demand" (Enz et al., 2010, p.18). This statement was given by Matthew Allard, who is the president and founder of Runtriz. Runtriz is the premier Los Angeles-based global hospitality network and has specialized in mobile solutions for the world's top hospitality and hotel brands. The company consists of ten employees, three board members and seven team members. (Runtriz, 2012a)

Allard was working several years in the hospitality industry and recognized existing service gaps within the day to day work in hotels. Even in the luxury hospitality, waiting queues in front of the concierge desks are existing or the quick and impersonal answering of questions, reliant on the high amount of guests per employee. Another important fact, Allard was recognizing, was the gap between the guests' expectations and the real service offered. Guests want to see certain things and not just hearing them from the employees. The spa offerings, the restaurant and its menu, these are examples, which have to be visible for the guest. Additionally, customers are often uncertain in choosing an unknown service or product, therefore former guest comments about offerings can be helpful for the decision making process of a customer. (Enz et al., 2010)

Allards was considering all those information he gained from his experiences in the hospitality industry and established the application named Hotel Evolution. The next chapter introduces and explains the application.

2.2 Introduction of the Invention Hotel Evolution

The beta-version of Hotel Evolution was the usage of fixed tablets with touch screens within the hotels. This version had two disadvantages for the hotels, which can be named as firstly, high hardware costs and secondly an inflexibility in the usage for the guests. Therefore, the product has been suited for the nowadays demand. Hotel Evolution can now be seen as a mobile touch screen platform, which allows guests to communicate and interact with the staff in the hotel. Meaning, the guest can order their favorite dish during the drive to the hotel or ordering a massage treatment, get directly after arriving etc.. The web-based platform can be used on or off the hotel via

3

Runtriz- The Leader in mobile Hospitality | Due Date
by Doreen Kupke | 17th of
October

Wi-Fi. Guests can use their own smart phones or laptops to use the application, in the following app, but hotels are also providing their guests with tablets if wanted. Hotel Evolution can be fully personalized and *"works closely with each hotel to understand their brand, guests, and operations so the technology works seamlessly with the property"* (Runtriz 2012b). Some hotels are providing the direct communication and ordering to different departments, e.g. housekeeping or restaurant. Others are working together with companies at the destination and providing special offers or information about the companies and their offerings at their hotel app. (Enz et al., 2010)

Clients of the company are luxury-hotels all over the world, like Ritz-Carlton, Caesars Palace or the Four Seasons (Runtriz, 2012c). The software is seen as a development in service and customer management and is fitting perfectly into the service of personalized and customized services in hotels of the luxury class. Usage and design of the software is done to total individualization, depending of the hotel and also of the different departments from the hotel. The hotel`s service reach can be extended through the application and the communication between guest and employee is getting faster and easier through Hotel Evolution.

The concrete innovation of Hotel Evolution can be seen in the extension of technology, communication, data collection and the hotels service reach within the day to day working base (Victorino et al., 2005). This novel way of communication enables the hotels to get huge advantages within the customer interaction and service providing. The extended use of technology fastens and easier the communication. Additionally, the hotel is gaining a huge volume of data from the guests. As main advantages of the product can be mentioned the:

- Enhancement of the guest experience and service process
- Increase and collection of guest data and knowledge
- Easy and on/ off communication with the guests

(Enz et al., 2010)

The next chapter presents the theoretical base for the latter case analyze.

3. Theory

3.1 Definition of Service Innovation

First, one has to define the term Service Innovation. There are different definitions of the term; the most fitting for the author of this report, focusing on the hospitality industry is from Verma 2008 cited in Enz (2012, p.187):

"Service innovation is defined as the introduction of novel ideas that focus on services that provide new ways of delivering a benefit, new service concepts, or new service business models through continuous operational improvement, technology, investment in employee performance, or management of the customer experience."

In the case of Runtriz, all the criteria from the definition are fullfilled. The implementation of Hotel Evolution was a novel idea for the hospitality industry and provided a new way to deliver extra value for the cutomer. The new service concept can be seen in the extended way technology was used in the hotels and the way of communication with the guests improved. Furthermore, Hotel Evolution has improved their features and usage over the years since it has been firstly brought to the market (Enz et al., 2010). Hotel Evolution can also be seen as an investment in the employee performance, because as mentioned before in chapter 2.1, the employees have more time to talk to the guests, instead of e.g. taking phone calls and additionally, waiting qeues are reduced. (Enz et al., 2010)

3.2 Service Innovation Models

3.2.1 Models from Gallouj and Weinstein

Gallouj and Weinstein (1997) are focusing during their article *Innovation in services* at six different types of innovation, named:

- Radical
- Improvement
- Incremental
- Formalisation
- Recombinative
- Ad hoc

The authors want to set a base for the interpretation of innovations in the service sector. To setting the base, different views of innovations are done and the six dimensions are defined in the article mentioned above. The type of innovation has to

5

be understood, to analyse the effects and outcomes of the specific innovation. Innovations in the service sector can be seen as different to those in the goods sector. The improvements and outcomes of innovations in the service sector are hard to measure, e.g. increase of customer satisfaction compared to those in the goods sector, e.g. sales revenue. To demonstrate the different effects, Gallouj and Weinstein (1997) are using different vectors and characteristics of products in their models. The work of Gallouj and Weinstein (1997) breaks with the differentiation of non-radical and radical innovations and allows a broughter view through the adding of certain characteristics and modes of product improvements. Gallouj and Weinstein (1997, p. 547) defining an innovation as *"any change affecting one or more terms of one or more vectors of characteristics."* The author of this report will describe the Radical and Incremental Innovations more in detail in chapter 4.1 and combine the theory with the chosen case of Hotel Evolution. Other theories regarding innovations in a Service-Dominant logic are given by Michel, Brown and Gallan in 2008 and will be outlined in the next chapter.

3.2.2 Models from Michel, Brown and Gallan

The authors, Michel, Brown and Gallan of the article *An extended and strategic view of discontinuous innovations: deploying a service-dominant logic* published in 2008 are focusing on discontinuous innovations and their emerge in certain companies. An innovation is defined by Michel et al. (2008, p. 61) as *"discontinuous if it (1) significantly changes how customers co-create value (value-in-use criterion) and (2) significantly affects market size, prices, revenues, or market shares (value-in-exchange criterion)."* Meaning, the innovation has to change the customers' usage behavior and also has to have an impact on certain financial and economical company factors. In chapter 4.3, the definition will be combined with the chosen example of Hotel Evolution. Furthermore, the authors are dividing the topic in two main dimensions. Firstly the dimension of the customer`s role and how an innovation can change the different roles of the customers, named as buyer, payer and user. Secondly the innovations are divided into the different firm´s value creation role described as embedding of operant resources into objects, changing the integrators of resources and reconfiguring value constellations (Michel et al., 2008). The change of the integrators can be seen as the changing of the integration roles from customers and firms.The reconfiguring of the value constellation can be seen in the relationship and correlation of multiple actors and resources. The aim is to co-create value depart from the normal value chain. The six different kinds of innovation are taken by an S-D logic point of view at the services offered. The authors arguing that by changing one of the customers role or the firm´s value creation role, an innovation can be defined. This focus on innovations is a more customized view as the one of Gallouj and Weinstein (1997). The author of the report wants to focus in chapter 4.3 on the embedding of operant ressources into objectives and combine this innovation theory with the chosen case.

4. Case Analyses

To explain the service innovation of Hotel Evolution more in detail, the next chapter outlines models transferred to and explained with the chosen case of Hotel Evolution. Within this chapter, the Service Innovation of the company Runtriz will be analyzed through the usage of innovation models from Gallouj and Weinstein (1997), also the innovation of the customers role and the innovation of the firm`s value creation role are discussed through the models of Michel et al. (2008).

4.1 Radical Innovation

Gallouj and Weinstein (1997, p. 547) are defining the term of radical innovation as *"denotes the creation of a totally new product, i.e., one defined in terms of characteristics unconnected with those of an old product."* Hotel Evolution can be seen as a Radical Innovation within the hospitality industry. One has to be carefull at this point, cellphone and touchscreen applications allready existed at the market but the specific usage of such applications was new for this certain type of industry. There was not such a service offering as Hotel Evolution before within the hospitality industry. A new system and way of communication was created through to Hotel Evolution, also complete working processes within the customer-employee communication system changed. The old way of communication via phone or mail has been innovated now through the direct communication via the hotel application. It was also new that guests have the possibility and complexability to see and discover services, products, activities etc. through pictures and directly can read other guest comments to certain offerings from the hotels. As mentioned from Gallouj and Weinstein (1997) the competences of the company are also effected by Radical Innovations. Hotels are now able to provide better and more detailed information

7

Runtriz- The Leader in mobile Hospitality | Due Date
by Doreen Kupke | 17th of
October

about their guests and can enhance the guest experience and satisfaction when using the new competences. (Enz et al., 2010) In the case of Hotel Evolution, the hotels are able to create detailed guest profiles, including the favorite dish, music, flower, massage etc. This is also leading to more focused marketing strategies and offerings with the right product for the right guest. Additionaly the sales and revenues increased through the direct and customized offerings and the usage of the gained guest informations. (Enz et al., 2010)

Through to a Radical Innovation *"the entire system [...] is transformed or, more precisely, a new system [...] is created"* (Gallouj & Weinstein, 1997, p. 547). A new system of communication and information gaining is created within the hospitality industry via Hotel Evolution.

4.2 Incremental Innovation

As mentioned in chapter 4.1, Hotel Evolution can be seen as Radical Innovation regarding the way of communication and providing guest information for the hotel. In this chapter a deeper look is taken considering the type of innovation regarding the extension of the service reach. One aspect of an Incremental Innovation given by Gallouj and Weinstein (1997, p. 548) is that *"the general structure of the system [...] remains the same, but the system is changed marginally through the addition of new elements [...]"* Regarding this statement of Gallouj and Weinstein (1997), Hotel Evolution can be analysed as an Incremental Innovation by the addition of certain characteristics or new elements. The structure of serving guests remains the same, if recognizing that the hotel staff is still serving the customer and the customer has to make the order for the sevice. But certain changes are done,"*this may involve for example, the addition of one or two new characteristics to a certain type of product, either by directly mobilising certain competences, or by adding new technical characteristics"* (Gallouj & Weinstein, 1997, p. 548). Keeping this in mind and looking at the concierge service offering in the hotels, Hotel Evolution shall not replace the concierge service, rather enhance the concierge service, decrease bottlenecks and easier the communication (Enz et al., 2010). Hotel Evolution can therefore be seen as adding new technical characteristics to the normal service offered in a luxury hotel. The new characteristic mentioned by the definition above is the implementation of technology to the service process. Thereby, novel elements are added to the customer-employee service process. (Enz et al., 2010)

4.3 Changing the Customer Roles and Firm`s Value Creation

According to the authors Michel et al. in 2008, Hotel Evolution can be seen as a discontinuous innovation from a Service-Dominant logic view. First, one has to describe Service-Dominant logic, in the following S-D logic. Within the S-D logic the customer is a co-creator of value (Michel et al., 2008). The customer perceives and defines the value of a service; this theory is based on the value-in-use. Meaning, the value of a certain service has to be co-created by the customers; otherwise, there will be no value created. (Vargo et al., 2008) To make it clear on the chosen service from Hotel Evolution, if the app is not used by the guests, to offer or not to offer the app, makes no difference for the guests and is creating no value either. Within the article *An extended and strategic view of discontinuous innovations: deploying a service-dominant logic* in 2008, the authors are defining two main dimensions identifying a discontinuous innovation. The first dimension is regarding the *change of the customers' role*. As outlined before in this chapter, in a S-D logic, value is created with the guest rather than for them. "*This co-creation of value requires that customers perform three different roles: users, buyers and payer*" (Michel et al., 2008, p. 61).

The user role is changed through the application in the way that guests in the hotels can use the tool to inform themeselves about activities within the hotel and are no longer dependent to the hotel staff. Guests can use the hotel app wherever they want and are no longer bounded to a specific place or hotel. The payer role also changed, in the way that the guests perceive e.g. an ipad for free to their normal room fee, to use Hotel Evolution. This can be seen as an additional offering to their normal payment. The buying process of services within the hotel also changed. Guests are free to book directly a certain service they require, e.g. a massage. Also they do not have to wait for making an order, instead the order can be done directly with the application and the guest do not has to hurry when ariving in the hotel, instead he or she can order their favorit dish on the way to the hotel. (Enz et al., 2010; Michel et al., 2008) Reminding the definition of a discontinuous innovation in chapter 3.2.2, Hotel Evolution can be seen as significantly changing the customers`roles.

Runtriz- The Leader in mobile Hospitality | Due Date
by Doreen Kupke | 17th of
October

The second dimension one has to consider is the changing of the firm`s value creation. As mentioned in chapter 3.2.2 the author of the report wants to concentrate on the embedding of operant ressources into objects, because it best fits with the case. Operant resources *"can be used to act"* (Vargo & Lusch, 2011, p. 184). Operant resources are including knowledge and skills from customers as well as employees (Vargo & Lusch, 2011). Taking the hotels as customers of Runtriz, Hotel Evolution is providing new and important information via the saving and collecting of guest data. Therefore, Hotel Evolution can be seen as embedding operant resources into objects. New know-how can be gained and the skills and knowledge of the hotels can be increased via this innovation. Another advantage of the application can be seen in effecting the revenues and sales positively (Enz et al., 2010). *"Hotel Evolution has been successful in all of its installations, as measured by direct revenue [...]"* (Enz et al., 2010, p. 18). This statement is leading us to the second criterion of discontinuous innovations, the value-in-exchange criterion, which can be also seen as fullfilled via Hotel Evolution.

Figure 1 summarizes the outcomes of chapter 4.3 and illustrates them shortly. To get a more detailed overview, the innovative customer co-creation is divided into the hotel as the customer and the hotel guest as a customer.

Figure 1: Changing the Customer Roles and Firm`s Value Creation

Innovative customer co-creation groups	Innovative offering	Change of user role	Change of buyer role	Change of payer role	Change of firm´s value creation Embedded operant resources
Hotel Guest view	• Touch screen application for a easier communication with hotel staff • Unique guest experience	Extended user role in information gaining and flexibility of the place of usage	Order and buying process are getting more flexible; service is coming to customer not the customer to the service	Additional free offering of the Hotel Evolution application and an appliance to use it	
Hotel view	• Touch screen application for a easy and fast communication with guests • Enhance the guest experience • Management tool for gaining customer data				Adding knowledge and skills into service and marketing processes in hotels through guest data collection and analyze

(Own illustration based on Michel et al., 2008, pp. 59-60)

5. Conclusion

As presented in the report, the developing and implementation of new innovative services and products is a fundamental part for companies to stay successful in the business and keep customers satisfied. The case of Hotel Evolution is showing the complexity of an innovation and also presented the different stakeholders involved in the innovation process. The report presents a theoretical base of the term Service Innovation, using the theory of Gallouj and Weinstein (1997) as milestone in defining Service Innovations more in detail and went away from the strict Radical and Non-radical description of innovations. A better view on the customer involvement and the different roles of companies within the innovation process is done through the theories of Michel et al. (2008). The combination of the chosen case with the elected theories is done in chapter 4. The outcomes of chapter 4 are showing that the founder of Hotel Evolution has successfully combined the existing gaps in the service offering of hotels and created a way to overcome such gaps through to the invention of Hotel Evolution. The improvement of Hotel Evolution and the highly personalization of the application are demonstrating the changing nature of innovations. Nowadays, Hotel Evolution can be seen as perfectly fitting in the luxury hotel service process.

(III) List of references

Chesbrough, H., 2011. *Open Services and Innovation: Rethinking your Business to grow and Compete in a New Era*. 1st ed. San Francisco: Jossey-Bass.

Enz, C.A., 2012. Strategies for the Implementation of Service Innovation. *Cornell Hospitality Quarterly* , 53(3), 187-95.

Enz, C.A. et al., 2010. *Cases in Innovative Practices in Hospitality and Related Services*.Cornell University, 40(4)

Gallouj, F. & Weinstein, O., 1997. Innovation in services. *Research Policy*, 26, 537-56.

Michel, S., Brown, S.W. & Gallan, A.S., 2008. An extended and strategic view of discontinuous innovations: deploying a service-dominant logic. *Journal of the Academic Marketing Science*, 36, 54-66.

Runtriz (2012a). *Runtriz the leader in mobile hospitality*. Available:

http://runtriz.com/#aboutus [2012-10-15].

Runtriz (2012b). *Runtriz the leader in mobile hospitality*. Available:

http://runtriz.com/#yours [2012-10-15].

Runtriz (2012c). *Runtriz the leader in mobile hospitality. Available:*

http://www.runtriz.com/#clients1 [2012-10-15]

Vargo, S.L. & Lusch, R.F., 2011. It's all B2B.and beyond: Toward a sysem perspective of the market. *Industrial Marketing Management*, 40, 181-87.

Vargo, S.L., Maglio, P.P. & Akaka, M.A., 2008. On value and value co-creation: A service systems and service logic perspective. *European Management Journal*, 26, 145-52.

Victorino, L., Verma, R., Plaschka, G. & Dev, C., 2005. Service innovation and customer choices in the hospitality industry. *Managing Service Quality*, 15(6), 555-76.